Be Smart About Credit

CREDIT AND DEBT MANAGEMENT

Kathiann M. Kowalski

BE SMART ABOUT MONEY AND FINANCIAL LITERACY

Enslow Publishers, Inc.
40 Industrial Road
Box 398
Berkeley Heights, NJ 07922
USA

http://www.enslow.com

This book is dedicated to my son, Christopher Meissner.

Library of Congress Cataloging-in-Publication Data

Kowalski, Kathiann M., 1955–
  Be smart about credit : credit and debt management / Kathiann M. Kowalski.
    pages cm. — (Be smart about money and financial literacy)
  Includes index.
  Summary: "Examines credit and debt, including the various forms of credit, how to use credit, smart ways to ma debt, and using credit wisely to build a strong financial future"—Provided by publisher.
  Audience: Grade 9 to 12.
  ISBN 978-0-7660-4282-7
  1. Consumer credit—Juvenile literature. 2. Debt—Juvenile literature. 3. Finance, Personal—Juvenile literature I. Title.
  HG3755.K665 2014
  332.024'02—dc23

                                        2013016585

Future editions:
Paperback ISBN: 978-1-4644-0507-5
EPUB ISBN: 978-1-4645-1262-9
Single-User PDF ISBN: 978-1-4646-1262-6
Multi-User PDF ISBN: 978-0-7660-5894-1

Printed in the United States of America
112013 Bang Printing, Brainerd, Minn.
10 9 8 7 6 5 4 3 2 1

Illustration Credits: Shutterstock.com.

Cover Illustration: Shutterstock.com (Abraham Lincoln) and Comstock / Photos.com (black suit).

Contents

Throughout the book, look for this logo 🐷 for smart financial tips and this logo 🐷 for bad choices to avoid. Also, don't forget to "Do the Math" at the end of each chapter.

Two Ways to Look at Debt

As a college student, Robyn B. loved using credit cards. They let her go out often with friends. They also let Robyn buy new clothes and travel during school breaks. By the time Robyn graduated, though, she owed almost $7,000.

Eventually, Robyn had to start to repay this money. Otherwise, she would face mounting fees, interest charges, and debt collectors. Now, Robyn had to scrimp and save. She made credit card payments. In addition, she had to pay for rent, food, gasoline, and other expenses. Robyn tells her story in a video on the Texas Guaranteed Student Loan Corporation "Adventures in Education" public service Web site.

Bad debt problems don't go away overnight. Suppose Robyn paid $300 per month and her interest rate was 18 percent. Paying off $7,000 in credit card debt would take twenty-nine months. If instead she paid only $200 per month, it would take fifty months—more than four years!

Three percent of college students carry credit card balances greater than $4,000, reports a 2012 Sallie Mae survey. More than 21 million students attended American colleges and universities that year, so that is more than 630,000 young adults!

The average amount of debt on a college student's credit card is $755, says the survey. Only 33 percent pay off outstanding balances every month. The other two-thirds incur interest and other fees.

Why Borrow?

Credit and debt can either help or hurt your financial life. Much depends on why, where, and how much you use them. Of course, how you follow through with paying matters, too.

A debt is a legal obligation to pay money. Americans' two biggest forms of personal debt are home mortgages and student loans. These types of debt help millions of people enjoy home ownership and going to college.

A credit agreement is a contract in which one party agrees to advance money for another. If you get a credit card, the company that issues the card agrees to pay when you present it at a store or for cash advances. In return, you agree to repay those funds, plus any interest or other fees. If you don't pay the bill on time, you owe more fees and interest.

Interest is a charge for the temporary use of money. Usually, interest is a percentage of the principal, which is the amount someone borrows. Fees are other charges for things, such as late payments or ATMs (automated teller machines). Credit card companies make money by charging interest and fees. Often, businesses that honor the card also pay a small percentage to the credit card company. In their view, credit cards boost customer spending.

Used properly, credit can be very convenient. Credit card holders rarely need to carry cash. Credit cards also make payments easier for air travel, hotels, online purchases, and some regular expenses.

Credit cards can ease temporary cash shortages, too. Suppose your car breaks down a week before payday. With a credit card, you can have repairs done right away. You would then pay when the credit card bill arrives.

Credit and debt are not available to everyone. Creditors want to know they can get their money back—preferably at a profit. Thus, companies investigate customers' creditworthiness. Creditors review applicants' credit history. For secured loans or credit agreements, they also investigate any property someone might surrender for failing to pay. If someone is a bad credit risk, he or she may be unable to get credit or a loan. Or, that person may have to pay higher interest or fees.

Learn about credit and debt now. You'll make smarter financial choices later.

Plan ahead. Save as much as possible for big-ticket items, such as college, a home, or a car. Every dollar saved is a dollar you won't have to borrow and pay interest on later.

Borrowing isn't a magic well for all your wants and needs. Sources of lending aren't always available. You eventually must pay back everything anyway.

Evaluate items you might borrow money for in comparison to other items in your budget. In general, limit debt to necessities that you can't otherwise buy with cash or savings.

Be Smart About Credit

Now it's your turn to "Do the Math." The end of each chapter features a math or word problem. Use what you learned in the chapter to help you answer the questions. The right math will help you make the right financial decisions.

Do the Math

Here are one year's costs for the state university you want to attend:

Expense	Amount
Tuition (resident)	$13,067
Dorm & Meal Plan	$10,596
University Health Fee	$862
Other Fees	$480
Books**	$1,438
Personal Expenses**	$4,130
Transportation**	$420
Total**	$30,993
**=estimate	

After talking with your parents, you estimate the following resources will be available:

Source of Funds	Amount
Savings	$8,500
Parents' Contribution	$11,900
Scholarship Award	$2,500
Summer Job	$2,250

1. If all expenses and resources are as shown, how much money would you still need?
2. Suppose you borrow that amount for each of the first three years of college, plus 112 percent of that amount for a fourth year. Not counting interest and fees, what would you owe?

Two Ways to Look at Debt

Kinds of Credit and Debt

While forms of credit and debt vary, some basic concepts apply to them all. The principal is the amount someone borrows. If you borrow $10,000 for college, the principal of the loan is $10,000.

Interest is the cost for using someone else's money. Credit card interest and other fees make up the card's finance charge. Suppose you charged a $500 plane ticket on your credit card with an 18 percent annual interest rate. If you only paid $200 when the bill came, you would owe interest on the remaining $300. You'd probably owe interest on new charges, too. Contract terms might also let lenders and creditors collect late fees or other charges.

The term is how long you have to pay back a loan. Generally, the shorter a loan's term is, the larger payments will be. The longer a loan's term is, however, the more interest you'll probably pay.

Credit vs. Debit Cards

Until 2009, credit card companies aggressively courted teens' business. They wanted teens to charge—full steam ahead! As credit card companies raked in profits, teens paid high interest and fees.

Pitches to students included direct mail offers, T-shirt giveaways, and other promotions. Aletha B. filled out her name and address to redeem a free sandwich coupon. The next week, a credit card arrived in the mail with a $2,000 credit limit. Less than a year later, *CNN Money* reported, the naïve teen was in debt.

The Credit Card Accountability and Responsibility Disclosure Act of 2009 (Credit CARD Act) now restricts credit cards for young people under the age of twenty-one. Most teens under eighteen cannot get credit cards in their own names. From then until age twenty-one, young adults usually need a source of income to get credit on their own.

Prepaid or secured credit cards are an exception for teens and college students under age twenty-one. For those credit cards, the cardholder keeps the credit limit in a bank account. If the cardholder doesn't pay on time, the credit card company can automatically take money from that bank account.

Another exception is to have a cosigner. Another person—usually a parent or guardian—is on the account with the teen or college student. Then both people are responsible for any charges.

Most credit card companies offer revolving credit. Each credit card charge adds to the cardholder's debt, up to the card's dollar limit. A college student's card might allow charging up to $500 or $1,000, for example. Payments make more of the credit limit available for borrowing again.

Suppose a college student charges $450 on a credit card with a $500 limit. That person can only charge $50 more before hitting the limit. If the cardholder pays off the $450, the $500 credit limit is available again.

Debit cards are not the same as having debt. Rather, using a debit card contract authorizes withdrawals from a bank account. If you "charge" $90 for new clothes, for example, the money comes out of your account as soon as you use the card.

Debit cards require you to track your spending carefully. Otherwise, you risk overdrawing your account and incurring fees. Debit card purchases also don't carry all the safeguards that credit card purchases do. On the plus side, debit cards provide some convenience for online shopping, travel, or other purposes.

Student Loans

A student loan is a form of term loan. You borrow funds for an approved educational program. The lender usually pays the funds directly to the school. You agree to pay back the loan according to the contract.

Student loans generally offer lower interest rates than other loans. The Free Application for Federal Student Aid, or FAFSA, lets college financial aid offices and banks or other lenders determine how much you need. It also determines how much of your loans qualify for lower rates under different federal programs.

For example, information on the FAFSA may show that you need $4,000 in addition to money from your parents and savings. Perhaps a bank or student loan company might lend you that amount at a special rate of 3.4 or 5 percent. If you wanted to borrow more, the rate might be 7 or 8 percent. This is just an illustration. Programs' actual rates vary from year to year.

As a rule, students may defer, or postpone, repayment of the principal while they are enrolled in school more than half time. Some student loans also allow deferred payment of interest.

Your college education is a serious matter. Your financial obligations to pay for college are serious, too. Be sure you understand all the loan's terms. In most cases, you will need to repay the loans and interest, regardless of whether you finish college or get a high-paying job. Young adults usually cannot discharge student loans in bankruptcy, either.

Some lenders might also ask parents to guarantee student loans. Then, if students don't pay after graduation, the parents must pay. Such loans can put financial and emotional stress on families if parents are stuck with the bills.

Mortgages

A mortgage is a security interest in real property. The property owner borrows money from a bank or other lender. If the property owner fails to pay according to the loan's terms, the lender may take the property in a process called foreclosure.

People often use mortgages when buying a home. Most home loans have long terms—anywhere from ten to thirty years.

In many cases, borrowers must make a substantial down payment of 10 to 25 percent of the purchase price. Loans guaranteed by the Federal Housing Administration (FHA) require smaller down payments. As of 2013, FHA minimum down payments were as low as 3.5 percent.

Other Types of Credit and Debt

People also borrow money for other purposes. Car loans help people buy cars. Home improvement loans let people expand or repair houses. Like mortgages, both types of loans are usually secured loans. If borrowers don't pay on time, lenders may take the collateral—the property that secures the loan. A car dealer might repossess a car, for example.

Loans and credit also help people start and run businesses. Depending on the circumstances, lenders may require collateral for such loans.

Still, other types of loans provide cash for a short term. Examples include payday loans from check-cashing services and refund anticipation loans from tax return preparers. Both loans typically have high interest rates.

Cosigning loans and guaranteeing credit arrangements or loans count as debt, too. Don't enter into either arrangement lightly. You may become fully liable if the other person doesn't pay on time.

On the flip side, having a parent cosign for your first credit card or car loan can help get credit you couldn't get on your own. If that happens, don't abuse the cosigner's trust. Make timely payments so that person won't have to pay your bills or get a lower credit rating.

Take an active role in managing credit and debt. Keep your financial documents organized. Review bills or other financial materials right away. Mark due dates on a calendar so you don't accidentally miss payments.

Tracking and paying bills on time will help avoid unnecessary fees and debts. These practices will also aid in overall budgeting and financial planning.

Paying the minimum on credit card bills is not the same as paying off your debts. A minimum payment of $20 on a $1,000 credit card bill may avoid late charges. However, you'll still owe $980, plus interest and any new charges. Even if you made no new charges, paying off the balance could take eight years. Over that time, you'd pay hundreds of dollars in interest!

Instead, aim to pay the full balance of all credit card bills within the grace period. You'll avoid interest charges. Meanwhile, you'll build a good credit record.

Do the Math

Terry uses a credit card to buy a computer at the college bookstore. The computer costs $500, including tax. The credit card charges 21 percent interest. The minimum monthly payment is the greater of (a) $20 or (b) interest plus 2 percent of the outstanding balance. If less than $20 is owed, the entire amount is due.

1. Suppose Terry does not charge anything else and makes only the minimum payments of $20 on time each month. Paying off the debt will take thirty-four months, and the total interest paid will be $163.32. What percentage would the total interest be of the computer's $500 purchase price?

2. Suppose Terry makes ten monthly payments of $50, plus one more payment of $54.39. If Terry makes all payments on time, the debt will be paid off in eleven months, and the total interest will be $54.39. How much less interest would Terry pay this way than if he paid just $20 per month?

The Costs of Credit and Debt

Interest is the most obvious cost for credit and debt. Calculating that cost isn't always obvious, however. Other fees and charges may apply, too. Understand all the costs of credit and debt so you can make smart choices.

Fixed vs. Variable Rate

A fixed interest rate stays the same for the term of a loan or credit agreement. The advantage of fixed rates for borrowers is certainty. Fixed rates lock in an interest rate. Borrowers know what their costs are and can plan accordingly. If rates fall a lot, they can consider refinancing the loan. As discussed later, refinancing involves costs, but it's sometimes worth it.

Variable interest rates can change. The lender still gets the going rate for interest, even if market conditions change. Borrowers may benefit by paying a lower rate at first. However, borrowers risk

having to pay more as rates rise. Both term loans and revolving credit agreements can have variable interest rates.

Mortgages and other term loan contracts with variable interest rates spell out what happens when rates change. In some cases, monthly payments go up if rates rise. For example, a $750 monthly mortgage payment might go up to $800. Other contracts might keep the same monthly payments but change how long the debtor must keep making those payments. A borrower might make the same $750 monthly payment, for example, while additional interest is added to the loan's balance. Then paying off the loan might take another year or more.

Most credit cards charge interest on the average daily balance. The card issuer calculates the average owed on each day of the billing period. It then multiplies that by the monthly interest rate.

Sometimes, the average daily balance includes finance charges from a prior billing cycle. Then the new finance charge will include compound interest—interest charged on the interest. Compounding makes credit cards' effective annual rate higher than the simple annual percentage rate. For instance, a credit card's stated interest rate might be 18 percent. Compound interest might bring the effective annual rate up to 21 percent.

Credit cards with grace periods let cardholders avoid new finance charges by paying off all amounts within twenty days or whatever the contract says. Smart consumers only use credit cards with grace periods.

Be Smart About Credit

Other Credit Card Fees

Interest isn't the only way credit card companies make money. Annual fees for having a card can range from $15 to nearly $300. An airline might charge $100 each year for a credit card that earns frequent flier miles, for example. Occasionally, the benefits might substantially exceed any annual fee. Usually, though, credit cards without annual fees offer better deals.

Low-use or low-activity fees are another trap. These fees impose charges on people who don't use credit cards very often. In effect, they encourage people to incur debt.

Watch out for credit card limits, because exceeding them will cost you. Suppose you charge $1,600 on a card with a $1,500 credit limit. Federal law says companies need your approval before letting you exceed the credit limit. You may think the credit card company is being nice if it lets you charge another $100 of charges. However, you could then owe a $25 fee. Going over the credit limit again within six months might cost another $35.

If you pay your bill late, watch out! As of 2013, companies can collect up to $25 as a late fee. Another late payment within six months raises the fee to $35. Meanwhile, finance charges mount up.

That's not all! Foreign transaction fees on credit cards might add 1 to 3 percent to purchases made abroad. Even "free" credit card rewards sometimes charge fees to redeem rewards, such as gift cards, or to reinstate points after missing a payment. If you pay for something, it isn't really free, is it?

Points, Fees, and Other Loan Costs

Mortgages also involve costs besides interest. Application fees and loan origination fees pay someone to review your application. There's another application fee for federal home loan guaranty programs, such as those for the FHA or Veterans Benefits Administration.

Appraisal fees let lenders learn how much property is worth. Inspection fees make sure any building's structure is sound and satisfies safety codes. A survey confirms the property's legal description. Title insurance protects the lender if someone else claims he owns rights in the property. Attorney fees and court filings can be extra. All these costs can run several thousand dollars. Homeowners usually must pay these costs at the closing—the time when the property sale officially takes place.

Lenders may also charge fees called points. Each point equals 1 percent of the loan's principal. Two points on a $100,000 loan would be $2,000, for example. In theory, points pay the lender's administrative costs in making the loan. In practice, points are another way that lenders make money.

In 2012, the Consumer Financial Protection Bureau proposed rules that would require lenders to give borrowers a no-point, no-fee option. The option's interest rate would build in costs that fees would otherwise cover. Then customers could compare costs from different lenders more easily.

In any case, do the math. Online loan calculators provide worksheets that can help. Consider all the costs and loan terms. Then decide what's best for your short- and long-term goals.

Whenever possible, avoid any mortgage or other loan with a prepayment penalty. Paying an extra one to six months' interest makes it harder to cut down outstanding debt.

Shop around before signing up for any credit card, mortgage, or other loan. Just as you'd compare prices and features for clothes, electronics, or other products, investigate the terms and true costs for credit and debt. Credit and debt are financial products. Try to get the best value for your hard-earned money.

Some credit cards waive the annual fee for the first year. That may sound like a good deal to earn airline miles or other rewards. But the thirteenth month's bill could charge you a $100 fee. That's usually not such a good deal.

Other credit cards offer low introductory rates. Maybe the annual interest rate for the first year is just 6 percent. You might run up charges but then find yourself owing an annual rate of 20 percent after the first year.

Read all the fine print before accepting any deal. Can you live with all the terms after the introductory period ends?

Be Smart About Credit

Do the Math

To finance their home, Kerry and Edward get a mortgage loan of $100,000. The fixed interest rate for their twenty-year loan is 6 percent a year. Payments are due in equal monthly installments of $716.43 for 239 months, with one final payment of $716.92.

This chart shows the loan's amortization over the twenty-year period. Amortization breaks down how much of each loan payment goes toward principal and interest. As the outstanding principal decreases over time, the interest share of each payment also goes down.

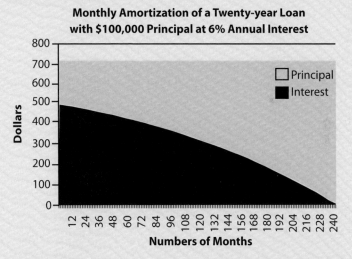

**Monthly Amortization of a Twenty-year Loan
with $100,000 Principal at 6% Annual Interest**

1. About what fraction of the first year's payments goes toward interest?
2. About how long will it take before a majority of each payment goes toward principal?
3. If Kerry and Edward make all payments on time without any prepayments, they will pay $71,943.69 in interest over twenty years. What percentage is that of the loan's initial principal?

Credit Ratings and Reports

Even if you don't currently have credit cards or loans, you'll probably need or want them sometime in the future. Get your financial house in order now, so you won't face unexpected glitches later.

What's Your Score?

Equifax, Experian, and Trans Union are the three main credit bureaus in the United States. The companies collect detailed information about people's credit history. They then calculate credit scores. Credit card companies and other potential lenders get these scores when they investigate your creditworthiness. Employers and property owners might also review your credit history.

Credit scores are also called FICO scores. Previously known as Fair Isaac Corporation, FICO developed the first computer software to analyze creditworthiness. FICO's credit scores range from 300 to 850. The higher the score, the more creditworthy someone is.

For most people, payment history makes up just over a third of the FICO score. A history of late payments hurts someone's FICO score. Nearly another third of the FICO score comes from how much people owe. Someone whose charges often approach his or her credit card limits is likely a higher credit risk.

The last third of the FICO score looks at several factors. A long credit history can boost someone's score. Conversely, many recent credit card applications can damage the score. Also, having many unsecured credit cards appears riskier than having a few credit cards and a secured mortgage or other installment loan .

How a FICO score breaks down

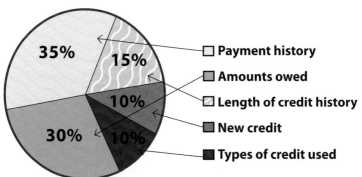

- ☐ Payment history
- ▣ Amounts owed
- ▨ Length of credit history
- ▤ New credit
- ■ Types of credit used

Of course, the final decision on any credit or loan application rests with each potential creditor. Besides your credit score, companies may also consider other factors, such as current income.

Check Your Report Card

Federal law lets you get one free credit report per year from each major credit bureau. Stagger requests every four months or so. Then you can check your credit situation three times per year, instead of just once.

Beware of TV and Internet promotions that require fees or memberships to get your free credit report. Use the Federal Trade Commission's (FTC) sponsored Web site instead: <www.annualcreditreport.com>.

Free credit reports usually don't include the actual FICO score, but they do contain important details about your credit history. That data includes your creditors and loans, payment history, and other information. Correct any errors right away. Even if there are no errors, see how your credit report stacks up against the FICO scoring factors.

Improve Your Score

Regular studying can help you do better on a pop quiz. Likewise, regular attention to your credit and debt situation can improve your credit score.

First and foremost, pay bills on time. A poor record marks you as a bad risk. The lower you can keep any outstanding balances, the better. Getting too close to your credit limit signals potential problems. Better yet, pay debts in full!

Resist the urge to move debts around from card to card. Using credit and debt isn't a shell game. Companies might offer low introductory rates if you transfer outstanding balances to new credit cards. However, those rates usually jump up after a short time. In any case, you still owe your debts and interest.

Apply for new loans or credit accounts only when you need them. You don't get points for having a wallet full of credit cards. Having fewer credit cards means fewer potential credit limits to max out.

If you have no credit history and limited income, consider getting a low-limit student credit card when you go to college. A $500 or $1,000 credit card would be enough to handle most emergencies or large necessary purchases, such as textbooks.

If you don't get a low-limit student credit card when you're in college, consider getting a debit card or secured credit card. Both options limit your spending to money in the bank. Be extra careful to avoid overdrafts and late payments.

Watch Out for Identity Theft

Identity theft happens when criminals use credit information and other personal data for financial gain. While identity thieves enjoy ill-gotten goods, you may find yourself left in the lurch. Bill collectors may pester you for crooks' debts. Meanwhile, crooks can ruin your credit rating.

The FTC fielded 279,156 complaints about identity theft in 2011. Eight percent of those cases involved teens. That's 19,563 young people who lost money or had to correct their credit history. You can't always prevent identity theft. However, you can make it less likely by following some guidelines:

- Keep private information private. Don't disclose your social security number, account number, or other financial data unless you know exactly who gets the information and why.
- Avoid easy-to-guess passwords. Use mixtures of uppercase and lowercase letters, numbers, and symbols.
- Use different passwords for different Web sites. Hackers have broken into many databases, including LinkedIn, Best Buy, Sony, and Yahoo! Contributor Network. When people always use the same password, identity thieves get more chances to commit fraud.
- Change passwords for e-mail and online accounts every sixty to ninety days.
- Shop or make payments only on secure Web sites.
- Don't fall for phishing expeditions. Any e-mail or phone call asking for your account number, social security number, or other personal information could be bogus. If someone raises a real concern, call back the phone number listed on your credit card or account papers.
- Don't share too much on social media. Your birthday, anniversary, pet's name, and other personal information can clue criminals into possible passwords.

Be Smart About Credit

GOOD ¢

Request your free credit report even if you don't have a credit card or other debt yet. Check for any credit cards, loans, or other accounts that you didn't open. If you see potential identity theft problems, act promptly:

- Notify law enforcement.

- Put a fraud alert in your credit files.

- Write to credit institutions or debt collectors about disputed accounts and charges.

- Review your credit reports regularly to follow up.

NON ¢

Don't fall for credit repair scams. Some companies may try to charge you for services that you could do yourself for free.

Even worse, some people may pressure you to break the law. Trying to erase accurate information in your credit history is illegal. Inventing a new credit identity is also illegal.

Do the Math

Pat's credit history shows the following:

- Buy! Buy! Revolving credit card since 2007 with three late payments per year. Current balance on the account is $5,899. Credit limit is $6,000.

- GasGoCo credit card since 2006 with all payments on time. Credit limit is $1,500 and current balance is $49.

- ShopMore, PayBuddy, and Bricks & Mortar revolving credit cards. Outstanding balances on these cards are $4,000, $4,400, and $4,800, respectively. Each card's credit limit is $5,000.

- Revolving credit cards issued within the last six months by ClassyStuff, Pampered, and Prestige stores with credit limits of $8,000 each. None of the cards has been used.

- Secured car loan with an outstanding balance of $2,000.

1. How much does Pat currently owe?

2. What advice might you give for improving Pat's credit score?

Know Your Rights and Responsibilities

Smart consumers follow the rule of *caveat emptor*: buyer beware! When it comes to money matters, watch out!

Shop around carefully. Read all financial documents and understand what you're getting into. If there's any doubt, don't use credit or incur more debt.

The Legal Landscape

Detailing all the law's requirements is beyond this book's scope. In general, the law provides some protection against predatory practices. That term includes many types of abusive, unfair, and fraudulent conduct. Hiking credit card fees without notice is one example. Misleading customers into buying unnecessary services, such as payment insurance, is another example.

The Truth in Lending Act and Regulation Z set out the main federal rules dealing with credit and loan agreements. The FTC, the Consumer Financial Protection Bureau, and federal banking authorities enforce the law. In general, all customers have basic rights:

- Lenders and credit card companies must provide detailed disclosures. Among other things, they must clearly state what the customer must pay and when. They must explain interest rates, fees, penalties, and other contract terms.
- Creditors must give notice if certain terms change.
- Creditors must state how customers can dispute charges.
- Creditors can use customers' confidential information only in certain ways.
- Creditors cannot discriminate because of factors such as race, religion, sex, national background, or marital status.
- Creditors face limits on whom they may deal with and what terms they can impose. For example, most teens cannot currently get unsecured credit cards in their own name.
- Creditors and collection agencies cannot improperly harass customers. For example, bill collectors can't call at all hours of the day and night.
- Subject to some exceptions, creditors cannot collect on debts that customers did not actually incur.

Unfortunately, the law does not enforce itself. Report any potential violations to the FTC or Consumer Financial Protection Bureau.

Be Smart About Credit

Do Your Homework!

Sadly, the law does not prevent people from making bad deals. Remember to consider all the costs of any deal, including tacked-on fees. Slick salespeople often sound like they're offering a great service. In fact, they're out to make a profit.

Get all promises in writing. Then read documents carefully. If you don't understand any deal, don't do it!

File all credit and loan information so it's handy. Keep hard copies of contracts, statements, and receipts organized in a safe place. Store any computer data only on removable media that no one else can access.

Review all billing statements promptly. If you need to dispute a charge, follow the creditor's procedures. Failure to do so could waive your rights and cost you money!

Call card issuers immediately if credit or debit cards are lost or stolen. Doing so preserves your rights and helps limit liability.

Never deal with a loan shark—a lender that operates outside the law. Loan sharks practice usury (unethical or immoral loans) by charging far more interest than the law allows. Even worse, they may threaten violence for late payments. Inform law enforcement immediately if anyone approaches you for such arrangements.

Do the Math

- As a smart consumer, you promptly review your latest PayU$ Credit Card statement and see two problems. (See statement shown on page 35.) First, you only dined once at Del's Deli on January 16. Your bill was $23.41.

- Second, you returned a defective video game to Big Box Department Store on January 8. The statement does not show the store's credit of $29.46.

- Write a letter contesting the errors to PayU$ Credit Card Company. State how much you will remit before the due date to pay the uncontested balance in full.

Be Smart About Credit

Pay U$ Credit Card Statement

Account Information		Payment Summary	
Account	123456789	Previous Balance (+)	$223.66
Name	Your Name	Payments/Credits (−)	−$223.66
Billing Period	01/02/16–02/01/16	Purchases/Debits (+)	$730.42
Statement Date	February 3, 2016	Finance Charges/Fees (+)	0
Payment Due Date	February 27, 2016	Cash Advances (+)	0
		Current Amount Due	$730.42
		Minimum Payment	$20.00

Reference	Transaction Date	Post Date	Description	Charges	Credits
xxxx11	01/02/16	01/05/16	Big Box Dept Store	$76.76	
xxxx22	01/02/16	01/05/16	Build It Yourself	$24.15	
xxxx33	01/03/16	01/05/16	Go Go Gasoline	$48.14	
xxxx44	01/07/16	01/08/16	Internet Provider	$15.00	
xxxx55	01/12/16	01/12/16	Tacky Taxi	$18.00	
xxxx66		01/14/16	PAYMENT		$223.66
xxxx77	01/16/16	01/18/16	Del's Deli	$23.41	
xxxx88	01/16/16	01/18/16	Del's Deli	$45.22	
xxxx99	01/16/16	01/18/16	Del's Deli	$30.66	
xxxx10	01/16/16	01/18/16	Del's Deli	$18.98	
xxxx20	01/23/16	01/25/16	FlyBy Airlines	$243.56	
xxxx30	01/25/16	01/26/16	Designer Duds	$186.54	

Know Your Rights and Responsibilities

Troubleshooting Tools

Chapter 6

Smart money management is the best way to avoid getting into financial trouble. Have a budget and update it regularly. Distinguish between needs and wants in your budget. Make paying for necessities a priority. If your budget doesn't balance, find ways to curb spending.

Schedule a weekly time to pay bills. Make sure your records reflect all automatic payments, check payments, and online transactions.

Beyond this, remember the most important rule for managing credit and debt: Never charge or borrow more than you can readily pay back! Don't spend more money for current expenses, including any long-term debt payments, than you have coming in.

If problems do crop up, don't ignore them! The more you let debt grow, the longer it will take to pay off.

A Nation of Debtors

Sadly, trouble with debt happens too often. As of December 2012, 46.7 percent of American households carried balances on their credit cards. Among those households, NerdWallet.com says, the average outstanding credit card debt was $15,325.

Delinquent debt can lead to hassles with bill collectors. Some creditors may also garnish wages. They can get your employer to pay them directly.

Nonpayment of secured loans can entitle creditors to seize collateral. On a car loan, for example, they might repossess the car. For home loans, creditors can foreclose on the mortgage.

Bad mortgage debts were one factor behind the financial crisis that hit in 2008. Many people had borrowed money on terms they couldn't afford. While housing prices kept rising, people kept refinancing their loans. After housing prices peaked in 2007, the bubble burst. Many people who couldn't refinance defaulted on their debts.

Meanwhile, banks and others had sold securities based on bundles of bad mortgage debts. As some businesses failed, companies became more reluctant to make loans. Many businesses' cash flow suffered. The economy slumped, and high unemployment followed. Thousands more people had problems paying their mortgages. Foreclosure filings exceeded 2.8 million in both 2009 and 2010. Banks repossessed more than 1 million homes in 2010.

By 2012, more than one-fourth of all mortgage owners were still "underwater," says the real estate database company Zillow. That means those homeowners owed more than their homes were worth. Even selling the home wouldn't pay off the mortgage.

Getting Help

Mortgage foreclosures cause massive upheavals for families. Yet all debt problems can become serious.

Suppose you were usually good about paying bills on time. Then a family member gets sick or you are laid off from a job. If a situation seems temporary, some companies may waive fees or change the payment plan.

In other cases, problems result from relying on credit and debt too often. If that happens to you, you need more than a payment plan. You also need to stop the bad practices that produced the problem.

The National Foundation for Credit Counseling has an online database of nonprofit organizations. Also, check out agencies with the Better Business Bureau.

Beware of anyone who guarantees you'll only pay pennies on the dollar. Also, avoid any agencies that ask for huge up-front fees or demand detailed financial data before saying what they can do.

Reputable credit counselors provide free information about the scope and cost of their services, their licensing and qualifications, and confidentiality. Get details in writing. If you can't afford the fees, see if the agency can modify them. If not, seek help elsewhere. Read everything before signing!

Be Smart About Credit

Credit counselors should help you review your budget. In some cases, they may also recommend a debt management plan. Basically, you pay money into an account. The credit counselor then pays creditors with those funds. In return for regular payments, creditors may reduce interest charges or waive certain fees.

Before agreeing, get assurance that the credit counselor will make all payments on time. Also, don't just take an agency's word that all creditors are on board. Double-check with your creditors. Unless they confirm their agreement, keep paying creditors directly.

Whether you use a debt management plan or not, don't expect business as usual for future credit card use. If you're facing huge debts, you probably should not use credit at all except for dire emergencies. New debts make it even harder to get back on track financially.

Bankruptcy—The Last Resort

If all else fails, consider personal bankruptcy. With some exceptions, the court takes jurisdiction over a debtor's property. Federal law determines which types of creditors are paid before others. The court distributes the debtor's property as far as it will go. The court then wipes out any remaining debts.

Bankruptcy is one way for debtors to get a fresh start. However, bankruptcy won't wipe out student loans and child support payments. The law also limits discharges of tax obligations.

In addition, debtors can't declare personal bankruptcy again for at least eight years. Home mortgage lenders and others are also more reluctant to make loans after people declare bankruptcy.

More importantly, a fresh financial start usually won't help unless financial habits change. For this reason, federal courts make everyone seeking personal bankruptcy go through credit counseling.

Of course, your best bet is to avoid trouble in the first place. Learn now how to budget and live within your means. That's the best way to avoid getting neck-deep in debt!

Resist people who urge you to "stretch" and incur extra debt for a pricier home, engagement ring, wedding, car, or other large purchases. You'll be paying the monthly bills—not them!

GOOD ¢

Don't let pride or denial delude you. Ignoring financial problems won't make them disappear. If you have a credit or debt problem, admit it and seek help.

NON ¢

Do the Math

Refinancing is taking out a new loan to replace an older one. In the right cases, refinancing can produce big savings. Lower monthly payments may be more manageable, too.

However, refinancing doesn't always make sense. Before making any deal, consider the costs.

Assume Kerry and Edward took out a twenty-year home mortgage loan of $100,000 with a fixed rate of 6 percent a year. After three years of monthly payments of $716.43, the outstanding principal on the loan is $92,255.77.

1. Suppose interest rates drop to 5.3 percent. If Kerry and Edward refinance at that rate for seventeen years, their new monthly payments will be $687.09. Suppose refinancing will cost 2 points—2 percent of the amount being refinanced—plus another $2,000. Calculate the refinancing costs. Should Kerry and Edward refinance?

2. Now suppose Kerry and Edward could refinance the outstanding balance of $92,255.77 with a fifteen-year fixed rate mortgage at 3 percent. The monthly payment would drop to $637.10. Assume the refinancing costs would be the same: 2 percent of the amount being refinanced, plus another $2,000.

Be Smart About Credit

a. How much lower would the monthly payments be if they refinanced?
b. How long would it take to recoup the costs of refinancing?
c. What other benefit would refinancing have if Kerry and Edward plan to stay in their home for many years?

Troubleshooting Tools

collateral—Property that secures someone's promise to repay a loan.

credit agreement—Contract in which one party agrees to advance money for another. Credit card agreements are a type of credit agreement.

credit history—Past performance under contracts for loans, credit cards, or other types of debt.

creditworthiness—Degree to which someone seems likely to pay creditors on time.

debit card account—Contract under which use of a debit card authorizes immediate bank account withdrawals.

foreclosure—Process by which a creditor may seize and gain title to property that secures a loan.

identity theft—Fraudulent use of someone else's personal information for gain.

interest—Payment or charge for the use of money, usually expressed as a percentage of the amount owed.

predatory practices—Abusive, unfair, or fraudulent business conduct.

principal—Amount of a loan or investment.

refinancing—Taking out a new loan to replace an older one.

revolving credit—Arrangement under which payments free up more of a credit limit for borrowing.

secured loan—Lending arrangement that lets a creditor seize property if the debtor doesn't pay on time.

term loan—Lending arrangement where someone must repay all amounts owed within a defined time.

usury—Unethical or immoral lending.

Learn More

Books

Butler, Tamsen. *The Complete Guide to Personal Finance: For Teenagers and College Students.* Ocala, Florida: Atlantic Publishing Group, 2010

Chatzky, Jean. *Not Your Parents' Money Book: Making, Saving, and Spending Your Own Money.* New York: Simon and Schuster Books for Young Readers, 2010.

La Bella, Laura. *How Consumer Credit and Debt Work.* New York: Rosen Publishing Group, 2013.

Lawless, Robert. *The Student's Guide to Financial Literacy.* Westport, Conn.: Greenwood, 2010.

Thompson, Helen. *Understanding Credit.* Broomall, Pa.: Mason Crest Publishers, 2011.

Internet Addresses

Bankrate.com: Educating Teens About Credit
<http://www.bankrate.com> Search for: "Teen" or "Teens"

CNN Money 101: Teaching Teens About Credit
<http://money.cnn.com> Search for: "Teen" or "Teens"

The Mint.org: Fun Financial Literacy Activities
<http://themint.org/>

Be Smart About Credit

Chapter 1: Two Ways to Look at Debt

1. The shortfall is $5,843: $30,993−$25,150 = $5,843.
2. The principal amount of the loans would be $24,073.16: (3 × $5,843) + (1.12 × $5,843) = $24,073.16.

Chapter 2: Different Kinds of Credit and Debt

1. To calculate how much the total interest is as a percentage of the purchase price, divide $163.32 by the $500 purchase price, and then multiply the quotient by 100. So, ($163.32/$500) × 100 = 32.7 percent, rounded to the nearest tenth of a percent.
2. Subtract $54.39 from $163.32, and the remainder is $108.93.

Chapter 3: The Costs of Credit and Debt

1. The answer is 5/7. For the first year, payments are approximately $700 per month, and the interest portion of each payment is roughly $500. 500/700 equals 5/7.
2. Hold a straight edge parallel to the x-axis around where $358 would fall on the y-axis. The straight edge intersects the curve at a point above the x-axis about three-fourths of the way between 96 months and 108 months. Divide by 12 months for each year. The answer is 8.75, or almost 9 years.
3. Divide $71,943.69 by $100,000, and multiply the quotient by 100 to get the answer: 71.9 percent. This problem does not consider any fees or points Kerry and Edward may have paid to get the mortgage loan.

Chapter 4: Credit Ratings and Reports

1. Add the current balances for each credit card and loan: $5,899 + $49 + $4,000 + $4,400 + $4,800 + $2000 = $21,148
2. Advice will vary, but should include: (a) paying all bills on time; (b) reducing the outstanding credit card balances; and (c) waiting before applying for more loans or credit.

Chapter 5: Know Your Rights and Responsibilities

The letter should use a business format. It should include your name, address, the date, account number, and date of the disputed statement. Then it should briefly explain the reasons for the three disputed charges from Del's Deli. It should also note the credit of $29.46 for the returned video game. State that you're enclosing copies of relevant receipts. Also, note that you'll pay the undisputed amount of $606.10 by the due date to avoid finance charges.

Chapter 6: Troubleshooting Tools

1. Refinancing costs would be 2 percent of $92,255.77, plus $2000, for a total of $3,845.12. Monthly payments would be $29.34 lower, but divide $3,845.12 by $29.34, and you get 131 months. Divide by 12 to convert that time to years. Recouping the refinancing costs would take almost 11 years. Refinancing does not make sense.
2. a. Subtract $637.10 from $716.43. Monthly payments would be $79.33 less.
   b. Recouping $3,845.12 of refinancing costs would take 48.47 months—just over 4 years.
   c. The shorter loan term would save Kerry and Edward two years of monthly payments.

Index

Be Smart About Credit